Exodus
Freedom to Serve God

A six-session Bible study for individuals and small groups

By Antony Billington

licc.

"You yourselves have seen what I did to Egypt, and how I carried you on eagles' wings and brought you to myself. Now if you obey me fully and keep my covenant, then out of all nations you will be my treasured possession. Although the whole earth is mine, you will be for me a kingdom of priests and a holy nation." These are the words you are to speak to the Israelites.

Exodus 19:4-6

INTER-VARSITY PRESS
36 Causton Street, London SW1P 4ST, England
Email: ivp@ivpbooks.com
Website: www.ivpbooks.com

First published 2019

British Library Cataloguing-in-Publication Data
A catalogue record for this book is available from the British Library

ISBN: 978-1-78974-084-4
eBook ISBN: 978-1-78974-085-1

Typeset in Great Britain by Sublime
Print and production managed in Great Britain by Jellyfish Print Solutions

*Inter-Varsity Press publishes Christian books that are true to the
Bible and that communicate the gospel, develop discipleship
and strengthen the church for its mission in the world.*

*IVP originated within the Inter-Varsity Fellowship, now the
Universities and Colleges Christian Fellowship, a student movement
connecting Christian Unions in universities and colleges throughout
Great Britain, and a member movement of the International
Fellowship of Evangelical Students. Website: www.uccf.org.uk.
That historic association is maintained, and all senior IVP staff
and committee members subscribe to the UCCF Basis of Faith.*

Contents

10   **Making the Most of Exodus**

18   **Session 1** | Hearing God's Call (Exodus 3:1–17)

30   **Session 2** | Experiencing God's Deliverance (Exodus 12:1–13; 29–32)

40   **Session 3** | Trusting God's Provision (Exodus 16:1–26)

52   **Session 4** | Becoming God's People (Exodus 19:1–6 & 20:1–17)

64   **Session 5** | Building God's Dwelling-Place (Exodus 25:1–9 & 31:1–11)

72   **Session 6** | Encountering God's Presence (Exodus 32:7–14 & 34:4–7)

80   Further reading on Exodus

Features

28   *What is the outline of the book of Exodus?*

38   *How does Exodus fit into the Bible as a whole?*

50   *What kind of writing is Exodus, and how should we read it?*

62   *How should we handle the laws in Exodus?*

70   *Why is the tabernacle so important?*

The Gateway Seven

Exodus — Law

Ezekiel — Prophecy

Mark — Gospel

1 Peter — Letters

Proverbs — Wisdom

Revelation — Apocalyptic

Ruth — Narrative

The Gateway Seven Bible Study Series

We don't approach a novel in the same way we tackle a legal document. We don't read poetry in the same way we might read a letter from a friend. So, we don't read the 66 books of the Bible as if they were all the same kind of writing. Story, song, law, letter, and more, all make up the rich repository of writing that together is God's word to us.

For *The Gateway Seven* series we've selected seven books of the Bible that each represent a different kind of writing. The mini-features sprinkled through the studies, together with the questions suggested for discussion, invite you to explore each book afresh in a way that's sensitive to its genre as well as to the concerns of the book itself.

Each study engages with a different kind of writing. However, each one in the series has been crafted with the same central desire: to offer a gateway to a deeper love of God's word and richer insights into its extraordinary implications for all of life, Monday through Sunday.

'May your kingdom come – on earth as in heaven', Jesus taught us to pray. May your kingdom come in our homes and places of work and service. May your kingdom come at the school gate as well as in the sanctuary. May your kingdom come in the hydrotherapy pool, in the council chamber, on the estate, around the Board table. May your kingdom come as we learn to live our everyday lives as beloved sons and daughters, wondrously wrapped up in our Father's 'family business'.

Our prayer is that these seven distinctive books of the Bible will be a gateway for you to a richer, deeper, transforming life with God wherever you are – seven days a week.

Tracy Cotterell

The Gateway Seven Series Editor
Managing Director - Mission, LICC

Making the Most of Exodus

Introduction to Exodus
Freedom to Serve God

A murderous ruler, an oppressed people, a baby in a makeshift boat, a bush that burns but doesn't burn up, a series of incredible plagues, a nation walking through a dried-up sea, a mountain that shakes. No wonder the story told in the book of Exodus has captured the imagination of artists and film-makers down the ages, and has influenced countless liberation movements through history.

But its message is even more significant than might first appear. The story is pivotal on the biblical landscape. The book of Exodus tells of the events which form the foundation for understanding God, his plan of salvation, and the place of his people in his purposes. God brings his chosen people out of slavery in Egypt into service to himself, in order to display to the world his character and glory. And the book starts a path that leads ultimately to Christ, reverberating through the rest of Scripture in a way that continues to shape God's people today.

The driving theme of Exodus is the Lord's commitment – in keeping with his promise to Abraham – to make himself known to the nations, and to do so through us. The book shapes us because it allows us to see how our identity as missional followers of Jesus is bound up with our call by God and our relationship with others in the community of faith. It shows how he forms us through challenges in the journey along the way, as he invites us to trust him in all things. Above all, it speaks of his loving commitment to preserve us in order that we might be the means of bringing his blessing to all people.

Here's a book which calls us to recover the link between what we are saved *from* and what we are saved *for*. Here's a book in which we see how God not only delivers us from slavery but also makes it possible for him to dwell among us. Here's a book which helps us to grasp what it means to be liberated from slavery for service in the everyday contexts in which we find ourselves, and to honour the Lord as we do so.

With their combination of creative animation and careful narration, **The Bible Project** videos – freely available online – say a lot and say it well. Their '*Torah Series*' overviews the story of Exodus in two parts, and their Old Testament section has two additional videos outlining the structure and design of the book. Find the videos at thebibleproject.com.

Studying Exodus

———

This Bible study is designed to look at select passages
in the book of Exodus over six sessions:

Session 1 | Hearing God's Call (Exodus 3:1–17)

Session 2 | Experiencing God's Deliverance (Exodus 12:1–13; 29–32)

Session 3 | Trusting God's Provision (Exodus 16:1–26)

Session 4 | Becoming God's People (Exodus 19:1–6 & 20:1–17)

Session 5 | Building God's Dwelling-Place (Exodus 25:1–9 & 31:1–11)

Session 6 | Encountering God's Presence (Exodus 32:7–14 & 34:4–7)

You can work through each session on your own,
one-to-one, or in a small group.

If your church is covering Exodus in a sermon series,
this study is an ideal way to deepen your learning and
explore the implications of the passages for Monday to
Saturday life. Working through the sessions in a group also
encourages each person to share insights and stories of
how they have seen God at work in their own context.

Each group has its own way of doing things,
so the session plan is only a suggestion, not a rule.

Suggested session plan

---

1 Pray to open

2 Read the 'First Thoughts' section

3 Read the passage from Exodus

4 Work through the questions

The questions cover different areas – the session's main theme, what the Bible passage says and means, going deeper, and living out the passage. Many questions don't have 'right' or 'wrong' answers. It's important and helpful to hear insights from everyone in the group. Group leaders may want to pick out the most pertinent questions for their group to discuss.

5 Pray to close

Don't feel bound by these prayer prompts if your study has taken a different turn. Be flexible in responding to each other's needs.

Dotted throughout this guide are brief feature pieces on questions or issues related to the background and study of Exodus. Together with some real-life stories – lived examples of how God's word can be worked out in daily life – they offer insights to deepen our understanding of the book and its implications.

Names and identifying details of the stories in this book have been changed to maintain anonymity.

Participating in the study

Before each session, you might like to read the passage together with one of the features, and any explanation boxes or stories that accompany the session. After you meet, you might like to pursue some of the 'Going Deeper' questions on your own.

Use this space to

Note down one or two things that strike you. As you journey through the study, come back to these notes each time and reflect on what God has been teaching you.

My frontline

Before you start the study, reflect on your frontline using these questions. Your frontline is an everyday place where you live, work, study, or play and where you're likely to connect with people who aren't Christians.

Where is your frontline?

What's going on there?
Who's with you there?

What are you excited about or struggling with?

What opportunities or challenges are you facing?

Come back to this reflection throughout the sessions, praying and trusting that God will direct your ways through his word.

Reading the whole of Exodus on your own

⎯

With its 40 chapters, Exodus is one of the longest books in the Bible. The Bible study sessions take in some of the major milestones of the book, but we'll be able to appreciate them more if we know where they come in the flow of the story as a whole. Below is a suggested reading guide through the book of Exodus which lasts for six weeks. Each week has six readings (some of them are longer than others, so you may want to use the seventh day to catch up!) Read through each portion slowly. You may find it helpful to pause on a few sections which stick out as you read them, and ask the following questions:

- What does this passage say about who God is?

- What does this passage say about how God works?

- What does this passage tell us about what God does for his people?

- What are the implications of this passage for us as God's people?

- What might we want to pray as a result of reading this passage?

- What insights does it offer for our everyday lives?

Six-week reading scheme for Exodus

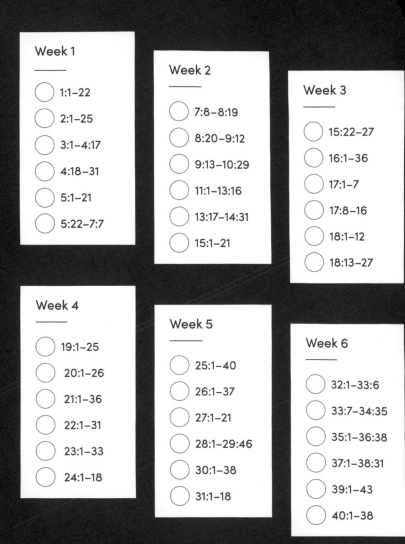

Week 1

- ◯ 1:1–22
- ◯ 2:1–25
- ◯ 3:1–4:17
- ◯ 4:18–31
- ◯ 5:1–21
- ◯ 5:22–7:7

Week 2

- ◯ 7:8–8:19
- ◯ 8:20–9:12
- ◯ 9:13–10:29
- ◯ 11:1–13:16
- ◯ 13:17–14:31
- ◯ 15:1–21

Week 3

- ◯ 15:22–27
- ◯ 16:1–36
- ◯ 17:1–7
- ◯ 17:8–16
- ◯ 18:1–12
- ◯ 18:13–27

Week 4

- ◯ 19:1–25
- ◯ 20:1–26
- ◯ 21:1–36
- ◯ 22:1–31
- ◯ 23:1–33
- ◯ 24:1–18

Week 5

- ◯ 25:1–40
- ◯ 26:1–37
- ◯ 27:1–21
- ◯ 28:1–29:46
- ◯ 30:1–38
- ◯ 31:1–18

Week 6

- ◯ 32:1–33:6
- ◯ 33:7–34:35
- ◯ 35:1–36:38
- ◯ 37:1–38:31
- ◯ 39:1–43
- ◯ 40:1–38

Session 1

Hearing God's Call

Exodus 3:1–17

First Thoughts

It's a story we've read or watched many times over: an unlikely hero undertakes a journey that is thrust upon them. Trials are endured, obstacles are overcome, friends are gained, sacrifices are made. Guided by a mentor, our hero becomes stronger and wiser along the way. Whether it's Luke Skywalker, Bilbo Baggins, or Katniss Everdeen, main protagonist of the *Hunger Games* trilogy, the 'hero's journey' has been told as long as stories have been told.

The significance of such stories shouldn't come as a surprise to Christians, for whom there is an Author who stands behind them, permeating them with his presence. All our stories of journeys and heroes, of sacrifice and redemption, speak of humanity's quest for identity, purpose, and hope, ultimately found in responding to God's call on our lives.

Our own adventure of faith won't necessarily involve dragons and death stars or their equivalents. The call to undertake a journey of discipleship is found just as much in the small moments of everyday life – in facing recurring fears, in doing difficult tasks, in submitting to God. As we do so, we discover that the one who calls us also equips us and promises to go with us.

Read – Exodus 3:1–17 👁

---

¹ Now Moses was tending the flock of Jethro his father-in-law, the priest of Midian, and he led the flock to the far side of the wilderness and came to Horeb, the mountain of God. ² There the angel of the LORD appeared to him in flames of fire from within a bush. Moses saw that though the bush was on fire it did not burn up. ³ So Moses thought, 'I will go over and see this strange sight – why the bush does not burn up.' ⁴ When the LORD saw that he had gone over to look, God called to him from within the bush, 'Moses! Moses!' And Moses said, 'Here I am.' ⁵ 'Do not come any closer,' God said. 'Take off your sandals, for the place where you are standing is holy ground.' ⁶ Then he said, 'I am the God of your father the God of Abraham, the God of Isaac and the God of Jacob.' At this, Moses hid his face, because he was afraid to look at God. ⁷ The LORD said, 'I have indeed seen the misery of my people in Egypt. I have heard them crying out because of their slave drivers, and I am concerned about their suffering. ⁸ So I have come down to rescue them from the hand of the Egyptians and to bring them up out of that land into a good and spacious land, a land flowing with milk and honey – the home of the Canaanites, Hittites, Amorites, Perizzites, Hivites and Jebusites. ⁹ And now the cry of the Israelites has reached me, and I have seen the way the Egyptians are oppressing them. ¹⁰ So now, go. I am sending

you to Pharaoh to bring my people the Israelites out of Egypt.' [11] But Moses said to God, 'Who am I that I should go to Pharaoh and bring the Israelites out of Egypt?' [12] And God said, 'I will be with you. And this will be the sign to you that it is I who have sent you: when you have brought the people out of Egypt, you will worship God on this mountain.' [13] Moses said to God, 'Suppose I go to the Israelites and say to them, "The God of your fathers has sent me to you," and they ask me, "What is his name?" Then what shall I tell them?' [14] God said to Moses, 'I am who I am. This is what you are to say to the Israelites: "I am has sent me to you."' [15] God also said to Moses, 'Say to the Israelites, "The LORD, the God of your fathers – the God of Abraham, the God of Isaac and the God of Jacob – has sent me to you." 'This is my name for ever, the name you shall call me from generation to generation. [16] 'Go, assemble the elders of Israel and say to them, "The LORD, the God of your fathers – the God of Abraham, Isaac and Jacob – appeared to me and said: I have watched over you and have seen what has been done to you in Egypt. [17] And I have promised to bring you up out of your misery in Egypt into the land of the Canaanites, Hittites, Amorites, Perizzites, Hivites and Jebusites – a land flowing with milk and honey."

Focus on the Theme ⊕

1. If you feel able to do so, share a time when you felt inadequate or unsuitable for a difficult task you needed to do.

What are some of the reasons we feel ill-equipped at such moments?

What was it that enabled you to go through with the task?

What Does the Bible Say? 🔖

2. Moses responds in several different ways to the appearance of God in the burning bush (3:2–6). How would you describe his responses?

3. How does God identify himself in Exodus 3:6?

Why might this be significant?

4. What verbs are used in Exodus 3:7–8 to describe why God is now acting the way he is?

How do they relate to what is said in 2:23–25?

5. What questions does Moses ask of God, and how does God respond (3:9–15)?

Going Deeper 🔍

6. Each section in the conversation between Moses and God includes a question from Moses or a reason why he can't do what God asks him to do, followed by a response from God. Glance through Exodus 3:10–4:17. What do we learn about God from the way he responds to Moses' anxieties?

7. Given the revelation of God's name in Exodus 3:14, what is the significance of Jesus' claims about himself in John 8:48–59?

God hears, remembers, looks, and knows

Exodus 1 and 2 cover a period of over 80 years. God is barely mentioned throughout the chapters, but a turning point comes in 2:23–25: 'During that long period, the king of Egypt died. The Israelites groaned in their slavery and cried out, and their cry for help because of their slavery went up to God. God heard their groaning and he remembered his covenant with Abraham, with Isaac and with Jacob. So God looked on the Israelites and was concerned about them.'

Spot the verbs. God *heard* – a hearing which acts on what is heard. God *remembered* – as he did with Noah (Genesis 8:1) and Abraham (Genesis 19:29). God *looked*, and God *was concerned*, or (as it could be translated) God *knew*. Some of the words are picked up in Exodus 3:7–9 when God speaks to Moses, and reaffirmed in 6:5 when God says: 'I have heard the groaning of the Israelites, whom the Egyptians are enslaving, and I have remembered my covenant.'

God delivers his people because he is committed to the promises he made to Abraham to reverse the impact of sin and its consequences. His 'hearing' and 'remembering' give the exodus a significance beyond the immediate predicament of the Israelites. What's being set in place is nothing less than God making good on his covenant with Abraham, and is a major step forward in his plan for the salvation of all nations.

God's name

When we introduce ourselves to others, we often start with our names. They mark us out even if they don't necessarily reveal much about us. In many cultures, however, names carry great significance, rooting us in a particular time, place, and family.

It's perhaps no surprise, then, that Moses anticipates that people will want to know the name of the God who sends him to them (Exodus 3:13). God identifies himself as the same God whom Abraham worshipped, locating himself in a story and relating what he is about to do to the promises he made to the patriarchs (3:6–10, 16–17; cf. 6:2–8). But his response to Moses' question about his name is enigmatic: 'God said to Moses, "I AM WHO I AM. This is what you are to say to the Israelites: 'I AM has sent me to you.'"(3:14)

The name relates back to God's promise to Moses in 3:12, where he says 'I will be with you'. His presence and his power will enable Moses to succeed. Indeed, the phrase in 3:14 could also be translated 'I WILL BE WHAT I WILL BE', suggesting that the actions he is about to undertake will show who he is. In part, we understand God's name – who he *is* – by what he *does*, which we discover as the story goes on.

Then, in 3:15, he reveals his name as 'The LORD'. The four Hebrew consonants here – YHWH – are sometimes written as 'Yahweh' (or 'Jehovah') in English. Most translations use 'LORD' (in small capital letters) for this special name of God, which appears more than six thousand times in the Old Testament. It as 'the LORD', the covenant God, that he delivers Israel from Egypt, in order to keep his promise to bless all nations.

Living it Out

8. God calls Moses even though he could easily deliver the Israelites himself. In the light of that observation, why is it significant that God chooses to work through his people then and today?

9. Think about different areas of your life, Monday through Sunday. In what ways does the dialogue between Moses and God encourage you in your calling to be a disciple in all of life?

Is there a specific area where you're learning to trust God at the moment?

10. Moses sees himself differently as a result of his encounter with God. Thinking about your everyday frontline, how has this passage helped you see yourself differently in this place?

In what ways has the session given you some fresh ideas about how you might be part of what God is doing there?

Prayer Time

Think about how God is portrayed in this passage and reflect on its significance for how we might pray.

- Thank God for what has struck you about who he is and how he works.

- God's calling is corporate as well as individual: ask for God's help in enabling you and the people in your church to 'live a life worthy of the calling you [plural] have received' (Ephesians 4:1).

- In pairs or as a group, share what you would like God to do in you and through you on your frontlines, in light of this session, and pray.

MARTIN'S STORY

He'd only just retired when the call came. It wasn't the call he wanted.

As Martin worked out his final couple of years, he and Myra thought and prayed a lot. 'How could we best use our time, skills, and experience in the service of God when retirement comes?' They were diligent, wise, and godly people. They saw ways they could enrich the ministry of their local church, serve on various boards, and commit time to charitable causes. There would be quality time together too: European riverboat cruises, evening strolls along deserted beaches, just time to be together.

With memories of his leaving-do still fresh in his mind, Martin noticed Myra was acting out of character. This intelligent and gracious lady started forgetting things, getting frustrated easily, just not quite being Myra. She was experiencing the early stages of posterior cortical atrophy, a form of Alzheimer's. And it got worse, quickly.

Decades before, Martin had looked into Myra's eyes and promised, 'in sickness and in health'. Now, with his sweetheart in the grip of this terrible disease, God called Martin to lay aside much of what they had planned, and to 'love and cherish' Myra, to care for her.

It was a calling that was as uncomfortable as it was unexpected. Because Myra had always taken care of the home, Martin had many new skills to learn: how to cook decent food, where to put the fabric softener, and how much.

It was a calling that required not just the development of new skills, but character too.

'It's a constant battle to get her fed, washed, and dressed... Then there's the maze of social services you have to work through. Drawing on the grace of God is absolutely essential, there's no two ways about that. Every day I pray for the compassion, strength, sensitivity, calmness, and the humility I need to look after her.'

How would you respond to a call you wouldn't choose?

As Martin followed this call, he found God to be faithful. Faithful in growing his character. 'I'm much more tolerant with other people when they make mistakes or bad choices. I have grown far more as a Christian in these circumstances than I would have done if this had never happened, although I wish I wasn't in this situation. I would like to think that my life is more Christ-like now than it was at the beginning of all this. I love God more and I love my neighbour more than I used to.'

God was faithful in working through Martin and Myra in the purpose of his mission to the world, too. Martin noticed how family members and former colleagues were more open to hearing about the difference God was making in his life. There were conversations with fellow carers, struggling with many of the things Martin was. He even got to talk about the transforming and sustaining grace of God to a room full of health professionals at an Alzheimer's conference.

Before Martin went to be with the Lord, his encouragement to those who respond to the difficult call of God was this: 'God loves you and he has not abandoned you; he wants to grow you through this time.'

What is the outline of the book of Exodus?

Exodus is a long book with many parts, and it's easy to get lost. But there are some basic divisions that are helpful to bear in mind, each of which brings out different dimensions of the book and its significance.

According to some schemes, Exodus can be divided into two main parts:

- Departure from Egypt (1–15)
- Journey to and arrival at Mount Sinai (16–40)

On this understanding, chapter 15 is a pivot in the book. Its song celebrating the crossing of the sea and the destruction of the Egyptian army looks *back* to what God has done in delivering his people, but also looks *forward* to what God will do in establishing his dwelling-place.

Others suggest a different twofold division, with the main break at chapter 18:

- Out of Egypt (1–18)
- At Mount Sinai (19–40)

Part of the problem with the simple twofold division is that the people leave Egypt in chapter 13 (though they aren't fully delivered until chapter 15), but they don't actually get to Sinai until chapter 19. So it's possible to see a middle or transitional section between Egypt and Sinai, with the people in the wilderness:

- Egypt (1:1–15:21)
- Wilderness (15:22–18:27)
- Sinai (19:1–40:38)

That division captures a sense of movement, allowing us to see that a journey is underway, that a transition is taking place. Each section also says something significant about God – as God reveals his power to his people and to Pharaoh in Egypt (1:1–15:21), as God provides for his people in the wilderness (15:22–18:27), and as God makes himself present with his people at Sinai (19:1–40:38).

More fully, then, an outline of Exodus looks like this:

1. Egypt – Power (1:1–15:21)

- Prelude: suffering in Egypt (1:1–7:7)
- Plagues: signs against Egypt (7:8–11:10)
- Passover: salvation in Egypt (12:1–13:16)
- Passage: safe from Egypt (13:17–15:21)

2. Wilderness – Provision (15:22–18:27)

- Provision of needs: water and food (15:22–17:7)
- Protection from threats: external and internal (17:8–18:27)

3. Sinai – Presence (19:1–40:38)

- The covenant made and confirmed (19:1–24:18)
- Instructions for the tabernacle (25:1–31:18)
- The covenant broken and restored (32:1–34:35)
- Construction of the tabernacle (35:1–40:38)

Session 2

Experiencing God's Deliverance

Exodus 12:1–13; 29–32

First Thoughts

The phrase 'expressive individualism' isn't exactly part of everyday speech, but it captures a significant dimension of everyday life. Understood as the free expression of an individual's natural desires and inclinations – the freedom to 'be myself' – it's a defining feature of our current age.

But it doesn't take too much to see such 'freedom' as illusory and even self-defeating. The freedom to play the piano or sail a yacht or operate a lathe – and to do so well – demands discipline, over many hours, submitting oneself to a set of practices, learning from others. Paradoxically, true freedom requires constraints.

Our society tends to see being free as freedom *from* certain obligations. But the biblical view is far richer. It's freedom *of* – the freedom of realising what we were designed to be, of loving and being loved, of experiencing joy and peace, of being set free from what used to enslave us. And it's freedom *to* – freedom to serve God and others. And it all comes about through the work of Christ, who sets us free to be free indeed (John 8:36).

Read – Exodus 12:1–13; 29–32 👁

---

[1] The LORD said to Moses and Aaron in Egypt, [2] 'This month is to be for you the first month, the first month of your year. [3] Tell the whole community of Israel that on the tenth day of this month each man is to take a lamb for his family, one for each household. [4] If any household is too small for a whole lamb, they must share one with their nearest neighbour, having taken into account the number of people there are. You are to determine the amount of lamb needed in accordance with what each person will eat. [5] The animals you choose must be year-old males without defect, and you may take them from the sheep or the goats. [6] Take care of them until the fourteenth day of the month, when all the members of the community of Israel must slaughter them at twilight. [7] Then they are to take some of the blood and put it on the sides and tops of the door-frames of the houses where they eat the lambs. [8] That same night they are to eat the meat roasted over the fire, along with bitter herbs, and bread made without yeast. [9] Do not eat the meat raw or boiled in water, but roast it over a fire – with the head, legs and internal organs. [10] Do not leave any of it till morning; if some is left till morning, you

must burn it. ¹¹ This is how you are to eat it: with your cloak tucked into your belt, your sandals on your feet and your staff in your hand. Eat it in haste; it is the LORD's Passover. ¹² 'On that same night I will pass through Egypt and strike down every firstborn of both people and animals, and I will bring judgment on all the gods of Egypt. I am the LORD. ¹³ The blood will be a sign for you on the houses where you are, and when I see the blood, I will pass over you. No destructive plague will touch you when I strike Egypt.

²⁹ At midnight the LORD struck down all the firstborn in Egypt, from the firstborn of Pharaoh, who sat on the throne, to the firstborn of the prisoner, who was in the dungeon, and the firstborn of all the livestock as well. ³⁰ Pharaoh and all his officials and all the Egyptians got up during the night, and there was loud wailing in Egypt, for there was not a house without someone dead. ³¹ During the night Pharaoh summoned Moses and Aaron and said, 'Up! Leave my people, you and the Israelites! Go, worship the LORD as you have requested. ³² Take your flocks and herds, as you have said, and go. And also bless me.'

Focus on the Theme ⊕

1. Think of how the words
'redeem' and 'redemption'
are used in everyday speech:

- 'He has no redeeming features.
  I don't know what she saw in him.'
- 'She didn't work hard in
  her first year at university,
  but she redeemed herself
  in her second year.'
- 'Clint Eastwood's *Unforgiven*
  is a typical Hollywood
  story of redemption.'

What other examples come to mind?

What Does the Bible Say? 🔖

2. Glance through Exodus
12:1–11. What, if anything,
strikes you as significant (or
interesting or puzzling) about
the instructions for Passover?

3. According to Exodus 12:5, what
kind of lamb was required, and
what is significant about this?

4. Why did God require a mark on
the door (12:7)? (Didn't he know
where the Israelites lived?)

5. Look at John 1:29, 1 Corinthians
5:6–8, 1 Peter 1:18–19, and
Revelation 5:6–14. In what ways
does the Passover point forward
to the rescue that Jesus brings?

Going Deeper 🔍

6. Read Matthew 26:17–30. What are the similarities and differences between the Passover feast and the last supper of Jesus with his disciples?

7. We tend to think of redemption in individual terms (being a redeemed person). What might be the significance of thinking of ourselves as a redeemed *community* (Titus 2:14, Revelation 1:5–6)?

The plagues

Although they're commonly known as 'plagues', they're actually called 'signs and wonders' in Exodus 7:3 (see also 4:21; 8:23; 10:1–2; 11:9–10). These acts of God make clear that what is being played out is not merely a contest between Moses and Pharaoh or even between the Israelites and the Egyptians, but between the Lord God and the gods of Egypt (12:12). Who is more powerful?

Some scholars suggest that individual plagues have specific Egyptian gods in their sights, calling into question their authority over (for instance) the Nile, livestock, and the sun. The last sign, the death of the firstborn, would be an attack on Pharaoh himself. In a culture where the father's inheritance was passed down through the firstborn son, a disruption of that line would be a threat to the throne of Egypt.

Through the mighty acts, both Egypt (7:5) and Israel (10:2) will come to know that the Lord is God, the sovereign creator, whose glory is seen in judgment as well as salvation.

Redemption

Israel's redemption from slavery models of an even bigger rescue – from slavery to sin and death. Echoing Passover, Peter writes: 'For you know that it was not with perishable things such as silver or gold that you were redeemed from the empty way of life handed down to you from your ancestors, but with the precious blood of Christ, a lamb without blemish or defect' (1 Peter 1:18–19).

Paul makes the link explicit when he says that 'Christ, our Passover lamb, has been sacrificed' (1 Corinthians 5:7). Elsewhere, he is clear that we're set free from one master into the service of another, to be 'slaves to righteousness' and 'slaves of God' (Romans 6:18–19, 22). Our release from slavery to sin frees us not to do as we please, but to enter service to God – a new Lord, a new way of living, and a new outcome – 'eternal life' (Romans 6:23).

The politics of deliverance

In the fourth century, Eusebius of Caesarea hailed the Emperor Constantine as a new Moses, deliverer of the persecuted church. In 2007, Barack Obama told black audiences that 'the Joshua generation' was ready to complete what 'the Moses generation' had begun.

In his fascinating book, *Exodus and Liberation: Deliverance Politics from John Calvin to Martin Luther King Jr.* (Oxford: Oxford University Press, 2014), John Coffey shows how Exodus has inspired visions of deliverance and empowerment on all sides of political divides. However, political re-readings of Exodus often miss the significance of the second half of the book. What's offered is not merely freedom from political or economic bondage, but freedom to a different kind of service to a different kind of king.

Living it Out (((•)))

8. Counteracting the fallout from the events of Genesis 3, Christ's death rescues us from guilt, shame, fear, and breakdown in relationships experienced by Adam and Eve. How do these factors impact you in your frontline context?

In what ways have you been most aware of God's redeeming power in this context?

9. Imagine: in conversation with a non-Christian friend, you get an opportunity to explain what Jesus' death means to you. How would you do so simply and succinctly using the idea of being set free from slavery?

10. How does the idea that God has released you from slavery into his own service affect how you see yourself and what you do in your everyday life?

Prayer Time ♕

• Take a few moments to reflect on what God has done in rescuing you.

• Give thanks that Christ, the Passover lamb, has been sacrificed, and that you have been redeemed – set free – from the penalty of sin and death.

• Ask that the redemption God has brought about through Christ would inspire you to live for him in your daily lives with deeper joy.

• Pray for a non-Christian friend or colleague who hasn't experienced the freedom Christ brings.

How does Exodus fit into the Bible as a whole?

Reading the first chapter of Exodus is like joining a movie part-way through. Indeed, the first word of the book in Hebrew is 'And', linking the story about to unfold with what has gone before.

In particular, the opening verses describe how the Israelites were 'exceedingly fruitful' and 'multiplied greatly' in Egypt (Exodus 1:7), taking us back to the beginning of the biblical story with the Lord's blessing on Adam and Eve to 'be fruitful and increase in number' (Genesis 1:28). The language also echoes God's promise of descendants to Abraham, and that all nations of the earth would be blessed through him (Genesis 12:1–3; 17:6; 18:18; 22:17–18). This being so, Pharaoh's action in oppressing Israel and in seeking to kill their baby boys stands in direct opposition to God's purposes for creation as well as the plan for his people to be a conduit of blessing to all nations. The grand stage on which the story of the exodus is played out is nothing less than God's great purpose to restore the whole world.

So significant is the exodus that memory of it plays a formative role in the worship and hopes of the people of God. It is remembered in their feasts (Exodus 12:14; 24, Deuteronomy 6:20–25; 26:1–11). It is cited as a reason for them to observe the sabbath (Deuteronomy 5:12–15). It is recalled with thankfulness as they look back at what God did for them (Joshua 24:5–7, 2 Samuel 7:22–24). It is sung about in their psalms (77:13–20; 78; 103:7–8; 105:23–45; 106:6–23; 135:8–9; 136:10–24).

It is also a cause for hope as the prophets draw on exodus imagery to describe the future deliverance of the people. Isaiah, especially, envisages the return of the exiled people from Babylon as like a new exodus (35:5–10; 40:3–5; 43:14–21; 48:20–21; 49:8–12; 50:2; 51:9–11; 52:10; 63:11–14). Jeremiah also promises that the people will experience an exodus-like deliverance from exile (16:14–15; 23:7–8), and looks forward to the day when a new covenant will be made with them in which the law will be written on their hearts rather than tablets of stone (31:31–34, cf. Ezekiel 36:24–28).

The reverberation of the exodus continues through the pages of the Bible into the New Testament as the gospel writers shape their stories of Christ and his significance around the exodus, and as the letter writers see the church – now made up of Gentiles as well as Jews – in the light of Israel's redemption from slavery. The contrast is not so much between 'physical' (Old Testament) and 'spiritual' (New Testament) as between promise and fulfilment. Whole-life liberation is in view in both testaments, as God makes good on his covenant promises to his people and his plan to bless all nations through them. As such, the pattern of redemption that begins in the book of Exodus is woven through the tapestry of the Bible as a whole.

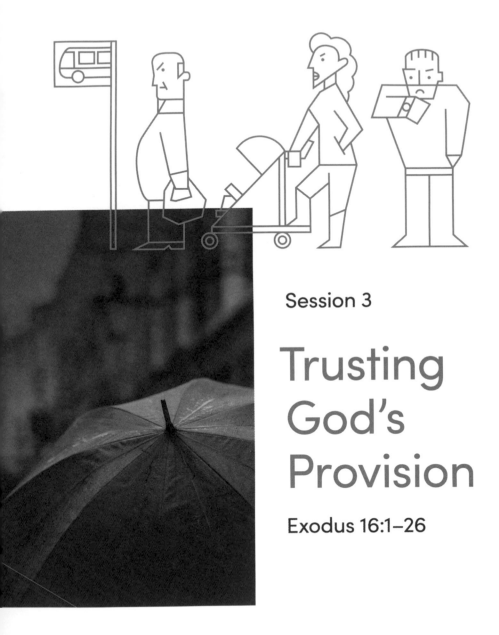

Session 3

Trusting God's Provision

Exodus 16:1–26

First Thoughts

'The beach was too sandy.' 'Noone told us there would be fish in the sea. The children were startled.' 'We had to queue outside with no air conditioning.' Stonehenge is 'just a bunch of rocks', the Mona Lisa is 'too small', and Machu Picchu is 'too high'.

You might recognise these as examples of complaints received by tourist operators from disgruntled holidaymakers. Indeed, complaining may well be among the top characteristics of British people – alongside queuing and talking about the weather! It's perhaps no surprise that grumbling has become a central aspect of online life, with social media providing endless ways to vent our frustration and dissatisfaction with everything from international politics to the local park.

But the propensity to grumble seems endemic to human beings across cultures and through history. That pervasiveness can give it the status of a 'respectable sin'. After all, we might think, it's not as serious as lust or greed or anger. Yet, on the heels of Paul's glorious telling of the story of Christ in Philippians 2:5–11, the first way in which Christians are to work out their salvation is to 'do everything without grumbling or arguing' (2:14). It's grumbling that prevents us from becoming 'blameless and pure', that stops us from shining 'like stars in the sky' (2:15). How did Paul know this? Perhaps he'd been reading Exodus.

Read – Exodus 16:1–26 👁

----

[1] The whole Israelite community set out from Elim and came to the Desert of Sin, which is between Elim and Sinai, on the fifteenth day of the second month after they had come out of Egypt. [2] In the desert the whole community grumbled against Moses and Aaron. [3] The Israelites said to them, 'If only we had died by the LORD's hand in Egypt! There we sat round pots of meat and ate all the food we wanted, but you have brought us out into this desert to starve this entire assembly to death.' [4] Then the LORD said to Moses, 'I will rain down bread from heaven for you. The people are to go out each day and gather enough for that day. In this way I will test them and see whether they will follow my instructions. [5] On the sixth day they are to prepare what they bring in, and that is to be twice as much as they gather on the other days.' [6] So Moses and Aaron said to all the Israelites, 'In the evening you will know that it was the LORD who brought you out of Egypt, [7] and in the morning you will see the glory of the LORD, because he has heard your grumbling against him. Who are we, that you should grumble against us?' [8] Moses also said, 'You will know that it was the LORD when he gives you meat to eat in the evening and all the bread you want in the morning, because he has heard your grumbling against him. Who are we? You are not grumbling against us, but against the LORD.' [9] Then Moses told Aaron, 'Say to the entire Israelite community, "Come before the LORD, for he has heard your grumbling."' [10] While Aaron was speaking to the whole Israelite community, they looked towards the desert, and there was the glory of the LORD appearing in the cloud. [11] The LORD said to Moses, [12] 'I have heard the grumbling of the Israelites. Tell them, "At twilight you will eat meat, and in the morning you will be filled with bread. Then you will know that I am the LORD your God."' [13] That evening quail came and

covered the camp, and in the morning there was a layer of dew around the camp. ¹⁴ When the dew was gone, thin flakes like frost on the ground appeared on the desert floor. ¹⁵ When the Israelites saw it, they said to each other, 'What is it?' For they did not know what it was. Moses said to them, 'It is the bread the LORD has given you to eat. ¹⁶ This is what the LORD has commanded: "Everyone is to gather as much as they need. Take an omer for each person you have in your tent."' ¹⁷ The Israelites did as they were told; some gathered much, some little. ¹⁸ And when they measured it by the omer, the one who gathered much did not have too much, and the one who gathered little did not have too little. Everyone had gathered just as much as they needed. ¹⁹ Then Moses said to them, 'No one is to keep any of it until morning.' ²⁰ However, some of them paid no attention to Moses; they kept part of it until morning, but it was full of maggots and began to smell. So Moses was angry with them. ²¹ Each morning everyone gathered as much as they needed, and when the sun grew hot, it melted away. ²² On the sixth day, they gathered twice as much – two omers for each person – and the leaders of the community came and reported this to Moses. ²³ He said to them, 'This is what the LORD commanded: "Tomorrow is to be a day of sabbath rest, a holy sabbath to the LORD. So bake what you want to bake and boil what you want to boil. Save whatever is left and keep it until morning."' ²⁴ So they saved it until morning, as Moses commanded, and it did not stink or get maggots in it. ²⁵ 'Eat it today,' Moses said, 'because today is a sabbath to the LORD. You will not find any of it on the ground today. ²⁶ Six days you are to gather it, but on the seventh day, the Sabbath, there will not be any.'

Wilderness training

After crossing the sea, but before their arrival at Sinai, is a period of about two months in which God provides for the needs of his people in the wilderness and protects them from threats (Exodus 15:22–18:27). Something of a rationale for the events of this section is offered in 15:25: 'There the LORD issued a ruling and instruction for them and put them to the test' (see also 16:4). The importance of following the Lord's instructions anticipates the commandments to come (including, in the manna episode, the sabbath – 16:22–30) and shows the people that their ongoing welfare will depend on their obedience to the Lord. While they were largely passive in the destruction of the Egyptian army, the encounter with the Amalekites (17:8–16) requires them to fight, showing that they will need to take a more active role in events going forwards. In short, the God who delivers his people also trains them, forming them into a 'holy nation' (19:6) who will obey him and represent him to a watching world.

Focus on the Theme

1. Think about grumbling. What sorts of things do you grumble about?

Who do you usually grumble to?

Why do you think you grumble?

How far does grumbling help?

What Does the Bible Say? 🏷

2. The people complain to Moses and Aaron about a lack of food (16:2–3), but in what ways are they also grumbling against God (16:6–9)?

3. How does God respond to his people's grumbling (16:10–16)?

4. How would gathering enough manna for one day at a time (16:17–18) and double on the day before the sabbath (16:22–26) foster trust in God?

5. In what ways did the people disobey God's instructions (16:19–20)?

Going Deeper 🔍

6. Look at Psalms 78:12–31 and 95:8–11. How do the psalmists describe the experience of the Israelites in the desert?

What is their 'take' on what was going on?

7. Look at some references in the New Testament to the wilderness experience of God's people – 1 Corinthians 10:1–13 and Hebrews 3:7–4:11. How do these passages fill out our understanding of this period in the life of the people of God?

Just enough

'Give me neither poverty nor riches, but give me only my daily bread.' So prays Agur in the book of Proverbs (30:8); but his 'just enough' principle is reiterated in different ways throughout the Bible. His request calls to mind God's provision of manna in the wilderness (Exodus 16), sufficient for the needs of the day, and it reaches forward to the petition for 'daily bread' in the Lord's Prayer (Matthew 6:11). Raising financial help for those suffering a famine, Paul draws on the manna episode in calling churches to give generously of their 'plenty' so that others who are hard pressed might be relieved (2 Corinthians 8:13–15).

The 'bread' for which we pray is given to us by a Father who loves us. Of course, we – along with farmers, bakers, and shopkeepers – do our bit to bring it into the house. But it's God who is the ultimate provider. And when we pray regularly, 'Give us today our daily bread', we remind ourselves of that.

The bread of life

In John 6:1–14, the feeding of the 5,000 takes place at a time when 'the Jewish Passover Festival was near' (6:4), in close proximity to Jesus saying that Moses wrote about him (5:46), along with instances of grumbling and murmuring (6:41–43, 61). Exodus bells should be ringing!

Indeed, following the miracle is a long dialogue and discourse about manna and bread (6:25–59). Jesus points to his own provision of bread in the wilderness as a sign of who he is: 'I am the bread of life. He who comes to me will never go hungry, and he who believes in me will never be thirsty' (6:35, and see 6:48, 51). Passover will no longer nourish them. What they need is the food 'that endures to eternal life' (6:27), which Jesus gives.

Living it Out ((o))

8. When you have found yourself grumbling at God, what do you think is at the root of your complaints?

How can we help each other remain faithful to God when we're tempted to grumble about his provision?

9. Given particular issues that you are facing at the moment, what might trusting God's provision for you look like over the next few weeks?

10. In Exodus 16:33–35, Aaron puts aside a jar of manna so that future generations could be reminded about the Lord's provision. What would you want to place in your own 'manna jar' as a reminder of how the Lord has provided for you?

Prayer Time 👑

- Use question 10 as a prompt to give thanks to the Lord for his patience, provision, and protection, even when you grumble!

- In pairs or as a group, share specific frontline situations, or reflect back on the issues you noted at the start of the studies. In light of what the passage in this session tells us about how God forms a people who will obey him, how might you pray for each other?

- Pray that you will trust his goodness in giving us 'our daily bread', and that you will not be tempted to hoard.

DAN'S STORY

Dan makes furniture. Beautiful, bespoke furniture.
His red brick workshop, nestled in the corner of his
garden, is adjacent to his kids' trampoline, and a metal
scooter with yellow squishy handles leans against it.
It was here Dan realised God really does provide.

You wouldn't know it from his craftsmanship, but Dan
never had any formal training. Much of his learning
comes from 'just trying stuff out', and from prayer. He
regularly finds himself saying to God, 'You are physically
going to have to help me with this.' Often, God obliges.

One day, Dan was trying to work out how to create a
metallic effect within those small crevices you get in the
knots of burr oak (as you do). The experiment would
involve melting some pewter (an alloy with a relatively
low melting point) in a pan. But Dan didn't have a pan.

With four kids, and his wife fully occupied with
them, money is pretty tight. Going out to buy a pan
he might only use once was not really an option.
Nor was half-inching a pan from the kitchen. Once
you've melted metal in a pan, you can't just wash it
up and use it to heat up the kids' spaghetti hoops.

Dan prayed. Sort of. 'I don't even know if I prayed
exactly, I had just said to God this is something I'd
like to do. I didn't need this for survival, it wasn't even
for a specific job I was working on – I just wanted
to learn a new process I could use in the future.'

How has God provided for you in the 'small things' of life?

Moments later, as he crossed the garden back to the house, he noticed something. On the other side of the low, weathered fence, was a skip. This wasn't unusual. Their house sits between a small industrial estate and a working farm, and the skip acts as a graveyard for deceased tractor parts.

On this particular day, lying atop dead starter motors and battered seats, was an old pan. It was exactly what Dan needed.

'God has provided for me so many times, but this incident particularly stands out. It was such a small thing, yet so specific. It was God saying "I love you and want to give you good things". It showed me that he was interested in a creative process I was working through. And he cared about me not taking something from the family in order to do it.'

He is our provider.
For I know the 'pans' I have for you, declares the Lord.

What kind of writing is Exodus, and how should we read it?

How we read depends, to a large extent, on what it is we are reading. The phrase 'Once upon a time' triggers a certain strategy for reading, while 'Dear Sam' or 'Roses are red, violets are blue' suggest a different approach may be required.

This being the case, what kind of book is Exodus, and how should we read it?

It's a book which claims to tell us something that happened in the past. But writing up events from the past inevitably involves selection in putting together a narrative with a beginning, middle, and end. Then, more than just a record of past events or even a great story, Exodus is clearly concerned to interpret the theological significance of the historical events in the account it tells. Like much of the Bible, the book of Exodus communicates its truth in three dimensions – through a combination of its historical background, its literary aspects, and its theological message.

Recognising the *literary* nature of the book means taking into account the story it tells, with all the conventions of good storytelling, where plot and characters are woven together in a narrative told from a particular point of view, which engages our imagination as we read. Exodus also incorporates other genres into its story – a poem (chapter 15) and legal material (chapters 20–24) – which add richness to the texture of the book. The song which celebrates the crossing of the sea (15:1–18) is no less 'true' than the narrative account of the same event which precedes it (14:1–31), but invites a different type of response. The narrative setting of the giving of the commandments in Exodus (19:4–6; 20:1–3) and elsewhere (Leviticus 19:33–36, Deuteronomy 1:1–5:5; 6:20–25; 15:15) is an important reminder that the law makes best sense in the light of God's prior action in saving his people.

Crucially, though, that action is rooted in *history*. That it is possible to make good sense of the book in the light of what we know about Egyptian customs of the time and ancient Near Eastern literature and law codes gives the book an authentic historical flavour. Although the Bible does not provide the precise date for when the events took place (the biblical and archaeological evidence can be interpreted in different ways), it is nonetheless clear that the events *did* take place. As with the resurrection of Jesus, if God didn't intervene in history on behalf of Israel, then their identity as a redeemed people lacks foundation. No exodus means no salvation and no hope.

So it is that from the *theological* angle, we can rightly ask what the book tells us about who God is, how he delivers his people, provides for them, makes a covenant with them, gives them laws, and allows a way of enabling himself to be present with them, so that his plan to bless all nations can be worked out.

Grounded in historical events, the book of Exodus – in the story it tells and the laws it contains – is written in a way that continues to speak with power to those who put their trust in the God of whom it speaks.

Session 4

Becoming God's People

Exodus 19:1–6
and 20:1–17

First Thoughts

Jordan Peterson is a Canadian professor of psychology who rose to fame in the UK through a now-famous interview with Cathy Newman on Channel 4, since viewed millions of times on YouTube. The interview no doubt helped with the sales of his book, *12 Rules for Life*, in which he offers self-help guidance of the tough-love sort. Most of his rules are to do with taking personal responsibility, making life choices that allow you to function well in the world. Such as: Rule 1 – Stand up straight with your shoulders back. Rule 3 – Make friends with people who want the best for you. Rule 6 – Set your house in perfect order before you criticise the world.

Whatever we make of Peterson's 'rules', having a 'rule of life' is more common than we might think, unavoidable even. In a sense, the issue is not whether we have a rule of life. It's more that we do, inevitably, live and work according to some set of guidelines, whether we acknowledge them or not. So, what's your rule of life? What's mine?

A rule of life is not just a set of disembodied rules, but a way of saying, 'This is how we live, because this is who we are, because this is who we belong to.' How you live depends on who you are, and who you are depends on who you belong to and of what story you are a part.

Read – Exodus 19:1–6 and 20:1–17 👁

¹⁹·¹ On the first day of the third month after the Israelites left Egypt – on that very day – they came to the Desert of Sinai. ² After they set out from Rephidim, they entered the Desert of Sinai, and Israel camped there in the desert in front of the mountain. ³ Then Moses went up to God, and the LORD called to him from the mountain and said, 'This is what you are to say to the descendants of Jacob and what you are to tell the people of Israel: ⁴ "You yourselves have seen what I did to Egypt, and how I carried you on eagles' wings and brought you to myself. ⁵ Now if you obey me fully and keep my covenant, then out of all nations you will be my treasured possession. Although the whole earth is mine, ⁶ you will be for me a kingdom of priests and a holy nation." These are the words you are to speak to the Israelites.'

²⁰·¹ And God spoke all these words: ² 'I am the LORD your God, who brought you out of Egypt, out of the land of slavery. ³ 'You shall have no other gods before me. ⁴ 'You shall not make for yourself an image in the form of anything in heaven above or on the earth beneath or in the waters below. ⁵ You shall not bow down to them or worship them; for I, the LORD your God, am a jealous God, punishing the children for the sin of

the parents to the third and fourth generation of those who hate me, [6] but showing love to a thousand generations of those who love me and keep my commandments. [7] 'You shall not misuse the name of the LORD your God, for the LORD will not hold anyone guiltless who misuses his name.

[8] 'Remember the Sabbath day by keeping it holy. [9] Six days you shall labour and do all your work, [10] but the seventh day is a sabbath to the LORD your God. On it you shall not do any work, neither you, nor your son or daughter, nor your male or female servant, nor your animals, nor any foreigner residing in your towns. [11] For in six days the LORD made the heavens and the earth, the sea, and all that is in them, but he rested on the seventh day. Therefore the LORD blessed the Sabbath day and made it holy. [12] 'Honour your father and your mother, so that you may live long in the land the LORD your God is giving you. [13] 'You shall not murder. [14] 'You shall not commit adultery. [15] 'You shall not steal. [16] 'You shall not give false testimony against your neighbour. [17] 'You shall not covet your neighbour's house. You shall not covet your neighbour's wife, or his male or female servant, his ox or donkey, or anything that belongs to your neighbour.'

Focus on the Theme ⊕

1. Think about how 'rules' operate in different spheres of life: household rules, rules in a school classroom, rules of the road. Why are such rules made, and how important is it to keep them?

What Does the Bible Say? 🏷

2. What has God done for his people, and what does he call them to do in response (19:4–6)?

3. Read Genesis 12:1–3 and Exodus 19:6. What is God's ultimate goal in selecting one person and people group from among the nations?

How is Israel's relationship with the Lord bound up with God's plan for the world?

4. Why is it significant that God begins with what he says in Exodus 20:2 before he gives the ten commandments?

5. In the commandments themselves (20:2–17), what is said about (a) how the people are to relate to God, and (b) how they are to relate to each other?

In what ways does Jesus' summary of the law in Matthew 22:34–40 reflect this two-fold dimension?

Going Deeper 🔍

6. Skim through the commands of the covenant in Exodus 21:1–23:33. What topics are covered?

What character traits of God are reflected in the laws?

7. Read Hebrews 12:18–29. What contrasts does the writer to the Hebrews draw between the experience of the people of God at Sinai and our experience as people of the new covenant in Christ?

The ten commandments: a charter for freedom

'Far from bringing about a new bondage, these commandments restored to the Israelites all that slavery in Egypt had damaged and destroyed – freedom from pagan gods, freedom to work with dignity and take time off, freedom to maintain proper family relationships, freedom to construct a framework of law and order, freedom to own houses and livestock and honour the ownership of others. The commandments were addressed in the singular to individuals in community, each one having the responsibility to maintain the conditions for all to flourish. And, since they had already been released from slavery, the commandments described the lifestyle of the redeemed, not the means of their redemption.'

Antony Billington, Margaret Killingray, Helen Parry, *Whole Life, Whole Bible: Journey through Scripture in 50 Readings* (Abingdon: BRF, 2012), 55.

Living it Out

8. How would you respond to someone who concluded from a reading of the commandments in Exodus that God is out to spoil our fun?

9. How do the values of the daily context in which you find yourself in any given week – your workplace or your neighbourhood or your leisure activity – overlap and/or divert from the ten commandments?

10. Having declared Christians to be 'a chosen people, a royal priesthood, a holy nation, God's special possession' (1 Peter 2:9), echoing Exodus 19:4–6, Peter calls on his readers to 'live such good lives among the pagans' (2:11). Thinking about one of your daily contexts – family or neighbourhood or place of work or study – what might this look like?

Prayer Time 👑

- Thank God for making you his 'treasured possession' (19:5), a 'kingdom of priests and a holy nation' (19:6), and for delivering you out of slavery (20:2).

- Pray for effectiveness as you take on your priestly role in neighbourhoods, workplaces, and families. Note down some specific prayers you can pray for one another and continue to pray these through the week.

- Pray that God would give each of you a renewed joy in loving God and neighbour as you go about your daily lives.

A priestly people

No more than a few months out of Egypt, the people gather at Sinai where God forms them into a nation, beginning to make good on his promise to bless all peoples. What role does God have for them in his plan? The answer comes in Exodus 19:4–6, which encapsulates the message of the book as a whole. These former slaves are told they have a privileged status as the Lord's 'treasured possession' and a special responsibility to be 'a kingdom of priests and a holy nation', representing God to the nations and the nations to God, a role they accept (19:7–8).

Following a series of commands given to the people (20:1–23:33), the terms of the agreement are repeated to the people twice, and twice they agree to obey (24:3–7). Then Moses sprinkles blood on them, declaring: 'This is the blood of the covenant that the LORD has made with you in accordance with all these words' (24:8). The application of blood to people is unusual. Its similarity to the consecration of the priests in Exodus 29:19–21 suggests that *all* the people are being commissioned into the service of the Lord – to be the priestly kingdom and holy nation spoken of in 19:6.

In the New Testament, Peter sees continuity between Israel's calling and what the church, now made up of Gentiles as well as Jews, is called to do (1 Peter 2:9–12). God's mission to bless all nations continues to be worked out through us, his chosen people, placed in the world for the sake of the world.

HARRIET'S STORY

As a pharmacist in an NHS hospital, Harriet's job is to make
sure patients get the right medicine, in the right quantity,
at the right times, and in the right way. She was good at
her job. For Harriet, there is no conflict of interest between
this role and her identity as a member of God's priestly
kingdom, called by God to help others get to know him.

In her first week on the job, Harriet was paired up with
another new starter, Daya. Daya is quiet and reserved, ten
years Harriet's senior, and was very committed to her Sikh
faith and temple. They got on really well, and it wasn't long
before Daya worked out that Harriet was a woman of integrity,
and that she genuinely cared. Daya opened up about some
challenges she was facing in her personal life, and Harriet
patiently and lovingly walked alongside her through these.

Both talked about their respective faiths, and asked each
other lots of questions. Daya would explain about the various
Sikh festivals and different aspects of temple life. Harriet
would talk about her understanding of God, what the Bible
says about him, and the difference he was making in her
life. For four years, conversations continued, the friendship
deepened, but nothing dramatic took place. Harriet longed
for Daya to encounter Jesus. She prayed for Daya a lot, and
would occasionally invite her along to events at her church.
Daya would usually say yes, only to cancel at the last minute.

Then one day, while eating their salads in the canteen, Daya
shared a dream she once had as a child. In it, she saw Jesus
over the whole world, with marks in his hands and feet, wearing
a crown. She even drew it for Harriet to see. Pretty amazing.
Yet another year passed, and nothing really changed.

Who are you persisting in prayer for?

One day, Harriet felt a nudge. A guest speaker was due to speak at her church, and she had a sense that if she invited Daya, this time she would actually turn up. So, she invited Daya, and she said she'd like to go. Sunday night arrived, and sure enough, Daya didn't cancel.

As Daya sat to her right, the preacher spoke about true forgiveness. Harriet was praying like mad, while also feeling slightly awkward, not knowing what Daya was making of it all. Partway through the service, Daya began to sob. Harriet didn't know exactly what was happening, just that something was happening.

When they spoke afterwards, with tears still in her eyes, Daya said, 'I've spent 30-odd years in the Sikh temple wanting to find God. I just sat here for an hour and a half, and I've met with Jesus.'

It wasn't long before family, colleagues, and friends recognised something had changed in the newly baptised Daya. She too was discovering what it meant to live out a priestly calling in her everyday life and work.

How should we handle the laws in Exodus?

Those who try reading the Bible from beginning to end often find the laws present the first real challenge. The Exodus story itself is gripping, and the ten commandments might be familiar, but then we're presented with regulations about household slaves (Exodus 21:2–11) and goring bulls (21:28–32), and told not to cook a young goat in its mother's milk (23:19). What are we to make of all this?

The section in Exodus 20:22–23:19 is sometimes called the 'covenant code' (see 24:7). In many respects, it's an expansion of the ten commandments applied to specific areas of the people's life together. While the ten commandments are phrased in the form of a direct command or prohibition ('You shall not...'), most of the laws that follow use phrases like 'If X happens, then do Y'. It's not a comprehensive law code. It addresses several issues that may arise between members of the community as they live together, much of it appropriate to the agrarian context in which the people of God found themselves at this time.

As Christians, we no longer build altars (20:24–26) or celebrate the three annual festivals (23:14–17). Nor is the temptation to boil a young goat in its mother's milk (23:19) high on our list of daily struggles. So, how should we handle the Old Testament laws for today?

Most important is to understand the covenantal framework of the law. 'I am the LORD your God' (20:2) reminds Israel that redemption comes before regulations, relationship before rules. The law is bound up with a commitment to serve their covenant Lord, to be a distinctive people, and to order their lives with each other appropriately – for the greater end of fulfilling their calling to be a priestly kingdom for the sake of the nations (19:4–6). While the new covenant changes the dynamics, the vocation to be a people set apart for God remains (1 Peter 1:13–16; 2:9–10), and with it the call to do things differently from those around us.

Although we no longer live under the Mosaic covenant, underlying principles in the laws – such as the call to holiness and the concern for justice – remain constant. Commands about goring bulls and straying oxen (21:28–36) might not be directly applicable in many of our contexts, but the broader principles carry implications for (say) how we handle our dogs or drive our cars, and encourage us to take an active role in looking out for the welfare of others. Laws about altars (20:24–26) and cooking young goats (23:19) were probably designed to prevent Israel from adopting pagan customs, and remind us of the danger of incorporating harmful practices into our lives.

For Christians, of course, Christ is key to how we understand the law. Far from setting aside the law and the prophets, Jesus carries them into a new era of fulfilment in which he governs our obedience (Matthew 5:17). He makes the same point in Matthew 22:34–40, where the law and the prophets are said to 'hang on' love for God and neighbour. The Old Testament law continues in full force for disciples of Christ, but – mediated through Jesus who fulfils it – its regulations are understood and embodied as expressions of love of God and of one's neighbour, worked out in every aspect of life.

Session 5

Building God's Dwelling-Place

Exodus 25:1–9 and 31:1–11

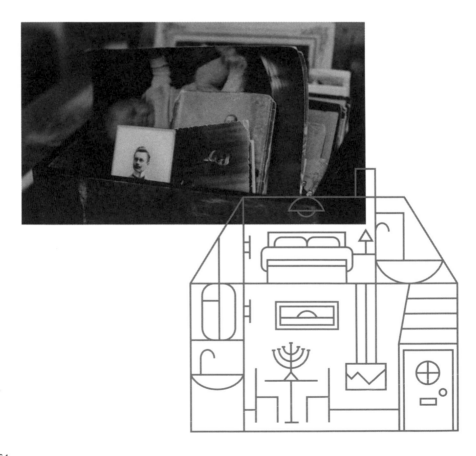

First Thoughts

Imagine: you make it through the stress of moving house only to be faced with the daunting task of what comes next. That wallpaper with the big orange flowers on the bright yellow background has got to go. The boiler is making a worrying noise and probably needs to be replaced before next winter. If you're more adventurous, you might knock through a wall or remove a fireplace. Slowly but surely, you make it your home.

Psychologists tell us that our homes capture the history of our habits and choices. Whether it's a room you rent or a house you've built, homes showcase our personalities and make statements about what matters to us – our goals, our values, our priorities. Traces of our character are captured in how the kitchen is organised, the child's drawing on the fridge, the knick-knacks we can't bring ourselves to pass on, in spite of all the advice from decluttering experts. What does your home say about you?

The Bible tells a story that makes sense of our longing for 'home', but makes it clear that the ultimate answer to that longing is found in the God who makes his dwelling with us. The tabernacle – how it was furnished and how it functioned – shows something of the God who chooses to dwell there: a place where provision is made for sin, a place which shows his commitment to relationship, a place which enables him to be present with his people, a place which provides a foretaste of the glory that will one day fill the whole earth.

Read – Exodus 25:1–9 and 31:1–11 👁

25.1 The LORD said to Moses, 2 'Tell the Israelites to bring me an offering. You are to receive the offering for me from everyone whose heart prompts them to give. 3 These are the offerings you are to receive from them: gold, silver and bronze; 4 blue, purple and scarlet yarn and fine linen; goat hair; 5 ram skins dyed red and another type of durable leather; acacia wood; 6 olive oil for the light; spices for the anointing oil and for the fragrant incense; 7 and onyx stones and other gems to be mounted on the ephod and breastpiece. 8 'Then let them make a sanctuary for me, and I will dwell among them. 9 Make this tabernacle and all its furnishings exactly like the pattern I will show you.

31.1 Then the LORD said to Moses, 2 'See I have chosen Bezalel son of Uri, the son of Hur, of the tribe of Judah,3 and I have filled him with the Spirit of God, with wisdom, with understanding, with knowledge and with all kinds of skills – 4 to make artistic designs for work in gold, silver and bronze, 5 to cut and set stones, to work in wood, and to engage in all kinds of crafts. 6 Moreover, I have appointed Oholiab son of Ahisamak, of the tribe of Dan, to help him. Also I have given ability to all the skilled workers to make everything I have commanded you: 7 the tent of meeting, the ark of the covenant law with the atonement cover on it, and all the other furnishings of the tent – 8 the table and its articles, the pure gold lampstand and all its accessories, the altar of incense, 9 the altar of burnt offering and all its utensils, the basin with its stand – 10 and also the woven garments, both the sacred garments for Aaron the priest and the garments for his sons when they serve as priests, 11 and the anointing oil and fragrant incense for the Holy Place. They are to make them just as I commanded you.'

Focus on the Theme

1. What does the place where you live – your rooms, your decor, your furniture – say about you?

How does it reflect your priorities, needs, and desires?

What Does the Bible Say?

2. Chapters 25–31 of Exodus detail the building of the tabernacle, a sanctuary for God. Why do you suppose there is so much detail?

What does this suggest about the significance of this episode in the book as a whole?

3. On what basis are God's people to make an offering towards the building of the tabernacle (25:1–2)?

4. What is the main reason for building the tabernacle (25:8, and see 29:45–46 and 40:34)?

5. Bezalel is the first person in the Bible who is said to be 'filled' with the Spirit of God (31:3). What does the task he is given to do say about the role of the Spirit in our lives?

What other qualities and skills does God give to the builders of the tabernacle (31:3–6)? Which, if any, are unexpected?

Going Deeper

6. Skim through the chapters in this section (Exodus 25–31), making a quick summary of what each section is about.

7. Read Hebrews 9:1–28, in which the writer describes the tabernacle as 'only a copy of the true one... heaven itself' (9:24). In what ways has Christ fulfilled the different elements of the tabernacle?

Living it Out

8. We have said that the first part of Exodus shows how God frees his people *from* slavery, but what does the second part (with building instructions for the tabernacle) say about what God frees us *for*?

9. How do the examples of Bezalel and Oholiab (31:1–6) encourage us to see how God fills us with his Spirit, wisdom, and understanding as we go about our daily tasks?

10. God dwells in us as his new covenant people (1 Corinthians 3:16–17; 6:19–20, Ephesians 2:19–22). How does knowing this affect how we view our frontline contexts and our witness to Christ in those places?

Freedom from Egypt, freedom to serve God

The book of Exodus has proved popular with filmmakers over the years, and it's easy to see why. It's a gripping tale, with strong characters, who play out a life-and-death drama. For many years, Cecil B. DeMille's 1956 version of *The Ten Commandments* was the definitive version of the story. More recently, Ridley Scott's *Exodus: Gods and Kings* uses the power of visual effects to make the most of the big screen. Or perhaps DreamWorks' animated version, *The Prince of Egypt*, is more to your liking!

However, most of the movies stop with the event itself – which ends up not doing justice to the overall thrust of the book. God rescues Israel from bondage and sets them free. But that freedom is not the freedom of autonomous individuals, free to do whatever they want. They've been freed from serving Egypt in order to serve God.

We see this in the word 'serve', sometimes translated as 'work' or 'labour', throughout the book. At the beginning, the word is used to describe the labour of the Israelite slaves in Egypt (1:13–14; 2:23; 5:9; 11; 6:6, 9). But then, as the book goes on, the same word is used for the service God asks of the people (12:25–26; 13:5; 27:19; 30:16; 35:24; 36:1, 3, 5; 39:32, 42).

One commentator summarises it like this:

'The book of Exodus moves from slavery to worship, from Israel's bondage to Pharaoh to its bonding to Yahweh. More particularly, the book moves from enforced construction of the buildings for Pharaoh to the glad and obedient offering of the people for a building for the worship of God.' Terence E. Fretheim, *Exodus*, Interpretation (Louisville: Westminster John Knox, 1991), 1.

Prayer Time ♔

- Reflecting on what we are freed *from* and freed *for*,
express your thankfulness to God together.

- Pray 'that Christ may dwell in your hearts through faith'
(Ephesians 3:17), transforming you more into his likeness and
a result so that the home where he is pleased to live.

- Offer the work of your hands to God – the work they will do, the support
they will offer to others, the talent they will exercise, how they will
represent your worship of God and your following of the way of Jesus.

Echoes of Exodus

The themes of the book of Exodus – the Lord's name, redemption,
sacrifice, provision, covenant, law, worship, presence – reverberate
throughout the Bible and find their ultimate fulfilment in Jesus.

The Bible utilises Exodus in ways that help us reflect on our
relationship with God. Stephen retells much of the exodus story in
Acts 7:17–44 in response to the charges brought against him by the
Sanhedrin. Paul cites instances from Exodus and Numbers, and tells
us that 'these things occurred as examples to keep us from setting
our hearts on evil things as they did' (1 Corinthians 10:6). The writer
of the letter to the Hebrews draws on the wilderness experience
(via its mention in Psalm 95:7–11) in calling his readers to obey God
(Hebrews 3:1–4:13). He also uses the example of Moses' parents,
Moses himself, as well as the people of Israel's passage through
the Red Sea in commending to his readers a life of faith (11:23–29).

The echos of Exodus throughout the Bible encourages
us to see that its examples and warnings might apply
to our own lives, as well as point to Christ.

Why is the tabernacle so important?

'Let them make a sanctuary for me, and I will dwell among them', God says to Moses. 'Make this tabernacle and all its furnishings exactly like the pattern I will show you.' (Exodus 25:8–9)

Exodus 25–31 records God's instructions for how the tent and its furnishings should be built, while chapters 35–40 describe their actual construction. The length of these sections and the repetition may feel dull to us, but they are significant for the movement of the story as a whole. God delivers his people in order to dwell with them (Exodus 29:45–46). Far from being an appendix, the book culminates here, with the Lord's glory filling the tabernacle (40:34).

The expression 'the LORD said to Moses' occurs seven times in the instructions for building the tabernacle (25:1; 30:11, 17, 22, 34; 31:1, 12), the final one of which is a command to observe the sabbath (31:12–18). Just as the week of creation finished with a day of rest, so the building of the tabernacle marks the completion of God's work of redemption. Like Eden, the tabernacle is a sanctuary where God will once again meet with men and women. The people who were formerly conscripted to work on building projects for Pharaoh now willingly bring offerings for the Lord's dwelling-place (35:21–29). In contrast to their earlier disobedience in the golden calf episode, they now do everything as the Lord commanded Moses (39:1, 5, 7, 21, 22, 29, 32, 42–43).

On the landscape of Scripture as a whole, the tabernacle is part of a trajectory that moves from the garden of Eden through Solomon's temple through Jesus to the new Jerusalem in the book of Revelation. John's description of the Word becoming flesh and dwelling among us and showing his glory (John 1:14) uses language which is reminiscent of the tabernacle. The letter to the Hebrews goes to great length in showing that the tabernacle, the priesthood, and the sacrificial system were 'copies of the heavenly things' (Hebrews 9:23), and 'a shadow of the good things that are coming – not the realities themselves' (10:1). Priestly ministry continues through the church, made up of Jews and Gentiles in whom God's Spirit now dwells (Ephesians 2:19–22, 1 Peter 2:4–10). All believers have access to God's presence through Jesus.

So it is that the climax of the book is not the crossing of the sea or the giving of the law, but the dwelling of God with his people, that they might become the means by which others are drawn to love and serve him. Within the scope of the book of Exodus as a whole – and the biblical story more widely – the Lord's presence with us is foundational for our mission to the nations, the purpose for which we are called.

Session 6

Encountering God's Presence

Exodus 32:7–14
and 34:4–7

First Thoughts

I remember it well. His eyes nervously scanning the audience, looking for me. And me, trying not to be too obvious, but sitting more upright than usual, hoping he'd catch sight of me. And when he did, such relief on his face and such a smile which spoke volumes – Daddy's here! It was a school assembly. Perhaps not hugely significant in the grand scheme of things but one where, on this occasion, my presence mattered.

Of course, living in a distracted culture, being present is easier said than done. It could be the sheer busyness of life, or the constant checking of messages and social media feeds on our devices. It could be the snatched conversations, half listening as we do the shopping or battle with traffic. The attentive engagement that accompanies genuine presence feels increasingly rare, and comes as a gift: the friend who just 'gets us', the teacher who listens for what's really bothering the teenager.

The biblical story begins and ends with the presence of God, which is both the means and the goal of our redemption. It is the goal in that we look forward to the day when he will dwell 'among the people' (Revelation 21:3). But his presence is also the means by which he fulfils that plan, making himself present in order to save us. We see it supremely in Jesus, 'God with us' (Matthew 1:23), who promises to be with us 'always, to the very end of the age' (Matthew 28:20). God delivers his people so that his presence might be at the heart of our lives together and for the world in which we live.

Read – Exodus 32:7–14 and 34:4–7 👁

32.7 Then the LORD said to Moses, 'Go down, because your people, whom you brought up out of Egypt, have become corrupt. **8** They have been quick to turn away from what I commanded them and have made themselves an idol cast in the shape of a calf. They have bowed down to it and sacrificed to it and have said, "These are your gods, Israel, who brought you up out of Egypt." **9** I have seen these people,' the LORD said to Moses, 'and they are a stiff-necked people. **10** Now leave me alone so that my anger may burn against them and that I may destroy them. Then I will make you into a great nation.' **11** But Moses sought the favour of the LORD his God. 'LORD,' he said, 'why should your anger burn against your people, whom you brought out of Egypt with great power and a mighty hand? **12** Why should the Egyptians say, "It was with evil intent that he brought them out, to kill them in the mountains and to wipe them off the face of the earth"? Turn from your fierce anger; relent and do not bring disaster on your people. **13** Remember your servants Abraham, Isaac and Israel, to whom you swore by your own self: "I will make your descendants as numerous as the stars in the sky and I will give your descendants all this land I promised them, and it will be their inheritance for ever."' **14** Then the LORD relented and did not bring on his people the disaster he had threatened.

34.4 So Moses chiselled out two stone tablets like the first ones and went up Mount Sinai early in the morning, as the LORD had commanded him; and he carried the two stone tablets in his hands. **5** Then the LORD came down in the cloud and stood there with him and proclaimed his name, the LORD. **6** And he passed in front of Moses, proclaiming, 'The LORD, the LORD, the compassionate and gracious God, slow to anger, abounding in love and faithfulness, **7** maintaining love to thousands, and forgiving wickedness, rebellion and sin. Yet he does not leave the guilty unpunished; he punishes the children and their children for the sin of the parents to the third and fourth generation.'

Focus on the Theme ⊕

1. In what moments or places have you felt a special sense of God's presence with you?

What Does the Bible Say? 🔖

2. Following the incident with the golden calf (Exodus 32:1–6), how does God describe the people (32:7–8), and what does he threaten to do with them (32:9–10)?

3. How does Moses respond to God in 32:11–14?

4. What words and phrases are used to describe God in 34:6–7?

How does God's description of himself match how he has dealt with his people so far?

5. Look ahead to the end of the story: in what ways does Exodus 40:33–38 provide a fitting climax to the book as a whole?

The suspense sin brings

If the holy God is to dwell with Israel, he'll need an appropriate place to live. Exodus chapters 25–31 contain lengthy instructions for that very purpose – to provide a way for God to be present with his people. But then comes a dramatic and terrible interruption to the story. Between the command to build the tabernacle (chapters 25–31) and the fulfilment of that command (chapters 35–40) is an account of the Israelites threatening the relationship between themselves and God by building and then worshipping a golden calf (chapters 32–34).

It's important not to skip too quickly from the instructions for building the tabernacle to its eventual construction without feeling the weight of the intervening section. Whether God will dwell with his people – or even let them survive – becomes a real question in the aftermath of their rebellion against him. How will the Lord respond?

The golden calf story serves as a warning about idolatry and provides a contrast with the surrounding sections. Only once restitution is made and the covenant is reaffirmed are the people allowed to proceed with the construction project, the climax of the book coming in 40:34–38 as the glory of the Lord fills the tabernacle.

Going Deeper 🔍

6. God's description of himself in Exodus 34:6–7 is repeated several times elsewhere in the Old Testament (just as a sample, see: Nehemiah 9:17, Psalm 103:8; 145:8, Jeremiah 32:18, Daniel 9:4, Jonah 4:2, Nahum 1:3). Why do you think God's people in subsequent generations keep returning to his self-disclosure here in Exodus?

7. John draws on Exodus language in John 1:14–18 (for example, 'made his dwelling' in 1:14 is reminiscent of 'pitching a tent'). In using words such as 'glory' and 'grace and truth', what points is John making about Jesus?

Living it Out 📶

8. How easy or difficult do you find it to be attentive to God's presence on your frontline, and why?

What difference do you think it would make to be more aware of God with you there?

How might you develop greater attentiveness to God on your frontline?

How could this group, or others, support you in this?

9. What aspect of God's character do you find most striking as it is revealed in the book of Exodus?

Why is it significant to you at this time?

10. If someone asked you what difference studying the book of Exodus might make to their everyday life, what would you say?

God's name (revisited)

Following the fall of the people into idolatry and Moses' pleading with God on their behalf, new stone tablets are formed, the covenant relationship is reaffirmed, and there is a further unfolding of the name of the Lord in Exodus 34:6–7: 'And he passed in front of Moses, proclaiming, "The LORD, the LORD, the compassionate and gracious God, slow to anger, abounding in love and faithfulness, maintaining love to thousands, and forgiving wickedness, rebellion and sin. Yet he does not leave the guilty unpunished; he punishes the children and their children for the sin of the parents to the third and fourth generation".'

This stands as the Bible's fullest description of the name and nature of God. Something of its significance is seen in the amount of times it is quoted or alluded to elsewhere in the Old Testament (Numbers 14:18, 2 Chronicles 30:9; Nehemiah 9:17, 31, Psalm 86:15; 103:8; 111:4; 112:4; 116:5; 145:8, Jeremiah 32:18, Joel 2:13, Jonah 4:2, Nahum 1:3). The statement holds together God's judgment along with his mercy, already indicated in the commandment about idolatry (Exodus 20:4–6) and demonstrated in the golden calf incident. Again and again, God's people confirm that the covenant is maintained with them only on the basis of the Lord's love, ultimately demonstrated in the one who lived among us 'full of grace and truth' (John 1:14).

Prayer Time ♕

- Read Exodus 34:6–7 and use the verses as a basis for prayer.

- Give thanks for how you've seen God at work in one another's lives through the time of this study.

- Give each person the opportunity to summarise one 'takeaway' and one ongoing prayer request from your Exodus study. In pairs, or as a group, pray for one another.

Epilogue

At the end of this study of Exodus, try to find a time when you can review the whole study prayerfully before God.

What was the most significant insight for you from the book?

What did you learn about reading biblical law?

Looking back on what was happening on your frontline when you started, how have you seen God at work?

Further reading on Exodus

The following list offers some further reading on Exodus for those who might like to dig deeper into the book.

Exodus
Teach the Text Commentary Series
T. Desmond Alexander
Grand Rapids: Baker Books, 2016

Exodus: God's Kingdom of Priests
Focus on the Bible
Allan Harman
Fearn: Christian Focus, 2017

How to Read Exodus
Tremper Longman III
Downers Grove: IVP, 2009

The Exodus Revealed: Israel's Journey from Slavery to the Promised Land
Nicholas Perrin
New York: FaithWords, 2014

Exodus: Saved for Service
Reading the Bible Today Series
Andrew Reid
Sydney South: Aquila Press, 2013

Other resources from LICC

Frontline Sundays
———

Five service plans with companion film shorts, sermon notes, activities, small group studies, and giveaways.

Imagine what would happen if every Christian looked around at the people they spend their days with and asked God: how do you want me to be good news to the people here today?

Frontline Sundays is everything a church needs to lead five Sunday services that will affirm, celebrate, and inspire the whole congregation for everyday mission, wherever they are.

licc.org.uk/ourresources

Fruitfulness on the Frontline

We all have an everyday context that's significant to God, full of people who matter to God.

Brimming with real-life stories, biblical insight, and practical steps, these resources shaped around our simple '6Ms' framework will spark your imagination and enrich your sense of wonder at the greatness and grace of the God who invites us to join his glorious work. The suite includes a book (for individual reading) and small group series (including videos).

licc.org.uk/ourresources

LICC Website

Whether you're looking to grow in your understanding of the Bible and its implications for your daily life, understand how to respond to the pressures and opportunities in today's world or workplace, or looking for resources to help you as you lead a whole-life disciple-making community, LICC's website is packed full of articles, videos, stories, and resources to help you on your journey. Sign up for weekly Bible reflections, blog posts, prayer journeys, and more.

licc.org.uk

About LICC

What difference does following Jesus make to our ordinary Monday to Saturday lives out in God's world? And how can we bring his wisdom, hope, grace, and truth to the things we do every day, to the people we're usually with, and the places we naturally spend time?

Vital questions in any era. After all, the 98% of UK Christians who aren't in church-paid work spend 95% of their time away from church, much of it with the 94% of our fellow citizens who don't know Jesus. Tragically, most Christians in the UK don't feel equipped to make the most of those opportunities. But what if they were?

That's what we at LICC are seeking to achieve. We work with individuals, church leaders, and theological educators from across the denominations. We delve into the Bible, think hard about the culture we're in, listen carefully to God's people, explore their challenges and opportunities... And we pray, write, speak, train, consult, research, develop, and test resources that offer the biblical frameworks, the lived examples, the practical skills, and the spiritual practices that enable God's people to know him more richly in their everyday lives, and grow as fruitful, whole-life followers of Christ right where they are, on their everyday frontlines, to the glory of God, and the blessing and salvation of many.

To find out more, including ways you can receive news of our latest resources, events, and articles, by email or post, go to licc.org.uk

licc.
The London Institute for
Contemporary Christianity